THE PATRIOTS AND THE POX

GEORGE WASHINGTON'S BATTLE TO SAVE THE CONTINENTAL ARMY

"I do not think my self equal to the Command I am honored with."

—George Washington,
commander in chief of the Continental Army, June 16, 1775

BETH ANDERSON

ILLUSTRATED BY
ASHLEY YAZDANI

CALKINS CREEK
AN IMPRINT OF ASTRA BOOKS FOR YOUNG READERS
New York

Leading the fight for independence from British rule weighed heavily on the new commander in chief. George Washington's mission to defeat King George III's mighty military force seemed impossible. And now he faced a mounting attack from *another* enemy.

It didn't wear red coats or carry muskets.

Didn't march with drums and fifes.

Stealthy . . . silent . . . unseen . . .

It invaded bodies.

Multiplied and strengthened.

Pain. Fever. Nausea.

A rash bubbled and oozed.

Itching. Burning. Stinging.

Smallpox!

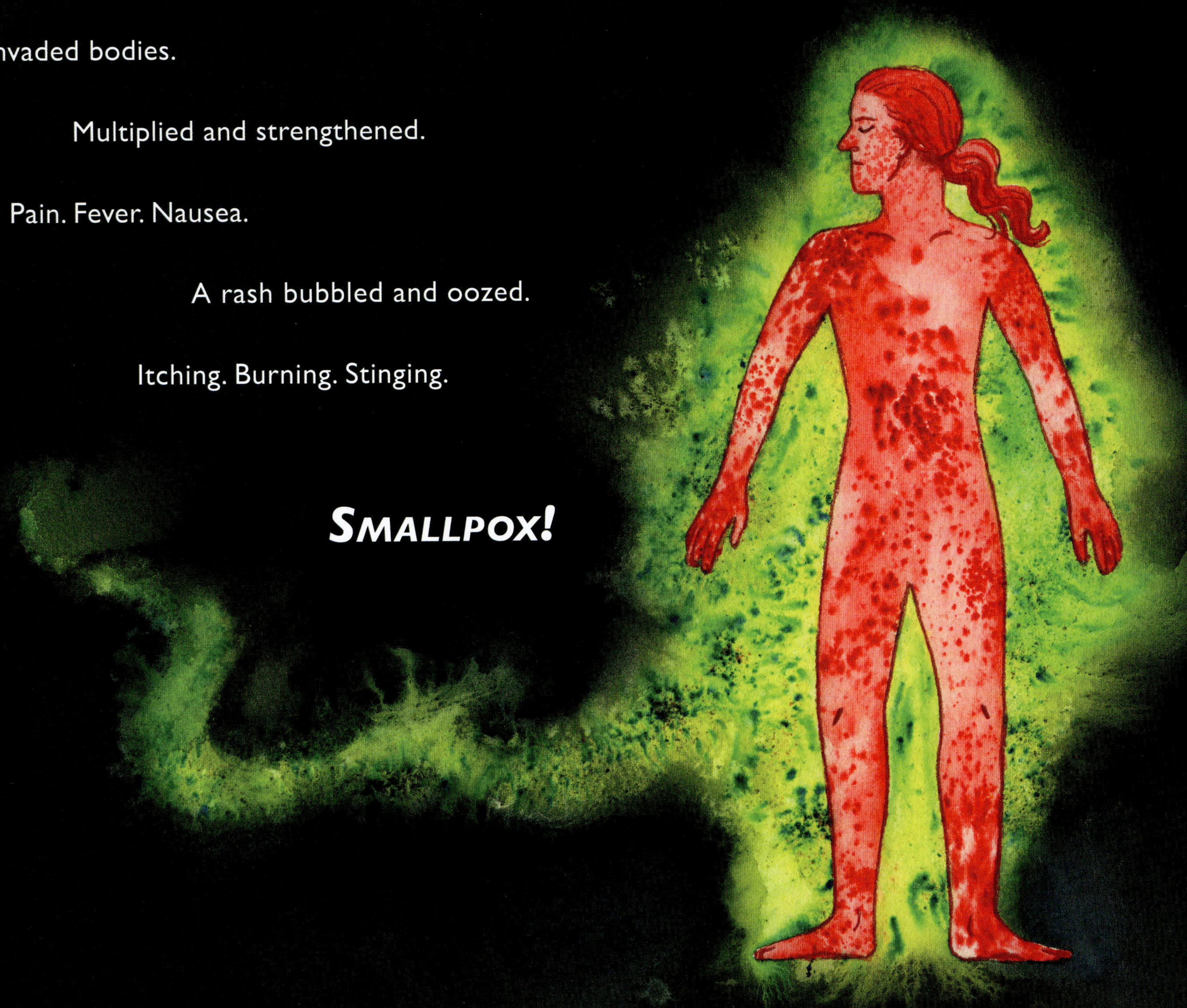

George understood the dangers of the disease—and the horrors. His pox-scarred face was proof he had immunity. He'd never suffer from it again.

Most of his men didn't have that protection.

But most of the redcoats occupying Boston did. After decades of smallpox epidemics in England, the virus raging in the city was little threat to them—instead, it was a weapon . . .

The thought terrified George. His men roaming around made easy targets. Smallpox could spread through his camps and kill a third of his troops.

He could lose his army before his first battle.

George put officers on alert.

For months George watched the British. When boats carrying infected colonists were sent out of Boston, his suspicions grew.

Were the redcoats using sick colonists to spread the disease?

The challenge of keeping smallpox out of camps worried him. But his other option—inoculation—was like opening the door and inviting the enemy in.

A drop of live virus inserted in a tiny cut usually caused a mild case of smallpox—enough to produce immunity. But the danger of spreading the disease came with it.

George would have to hospitalize inoculated troops for a month. If one careless soldier broke quarantine, the virus could spark an epidemic.

Inoculating his entire army was unthinkable.

From his headquarters outside Boston, George raised the alarm to his generals scattered across the countryside. But for his northern army, it was too late. Everything he feared was happening . . .

Smallpox blazed through crowded camps.

Panic erupted.

Soldiers disobeyed orders. Some men fled.

Others used virus from the sick to inoculate themselves. Without quarantine they fueled the fire of disease . . . spreading it further, faster.

News of the failure hit George like a cannon blast.

If George couldn't protect his army against smallpox, they'd never defeat the British.

The tragedy up north was proof he couldn't risk inoculating soldiers who didn't obey orders. Hundreds had died.

George needed men! Healthy men!

He doubled down. Isolation was safer. More controllable.

DISCIPLINE! QUARANTINE! NO INOCULATION!

HQ

In Boston, George's strategy worked.

His troops bombarded the British from a distance, then watched them sail out of sight.

George had a hunch where they were going and headed for New York City.

But nineteen thousand troops on the move made isolating against smallpox nearly impossible . . .

Long Island

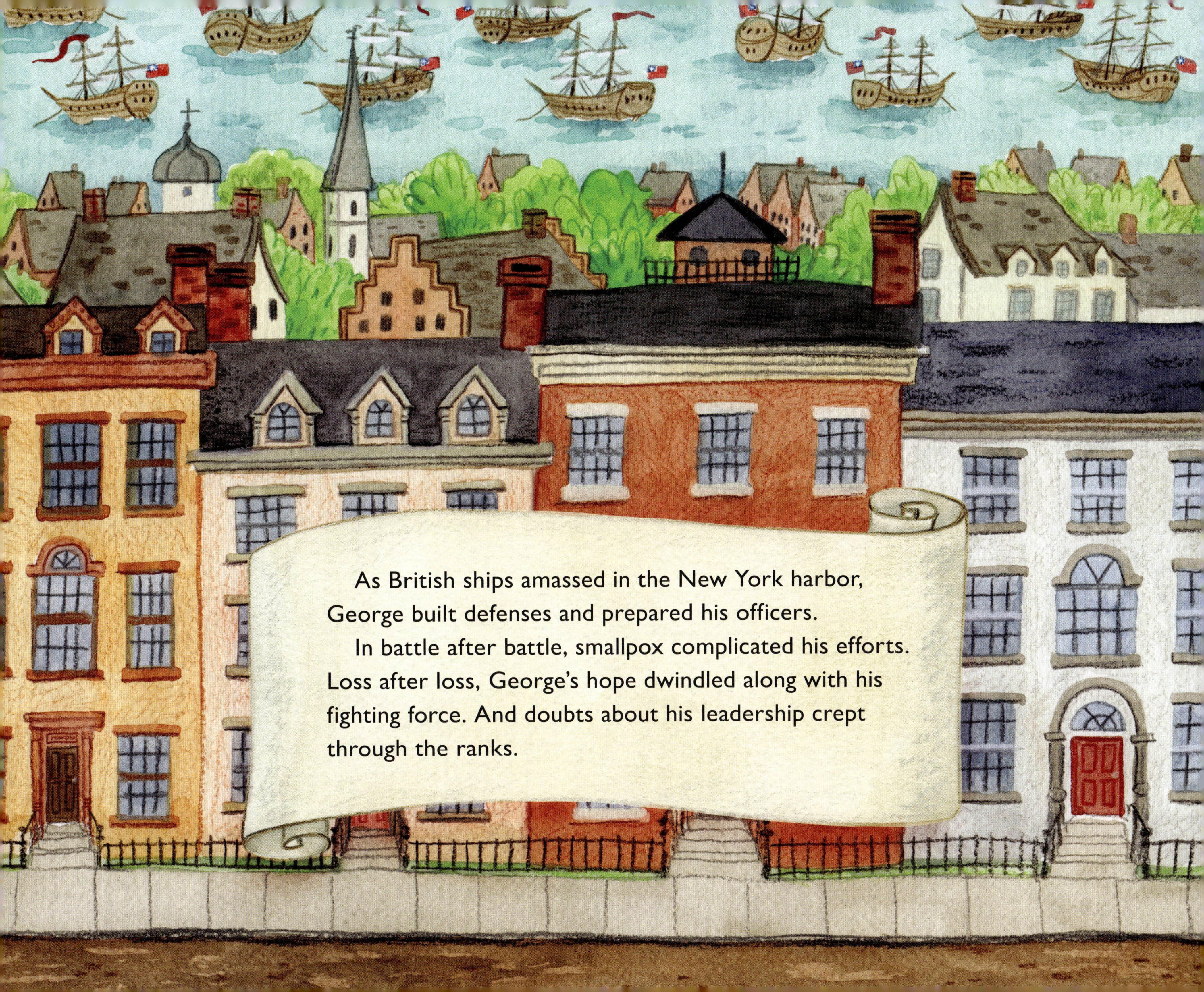

As British ships amassed in the New York harbor, George built defenses and prepared his officers.

In battle after battle, smallpox complicated his efforts. Loss after loss, George's hope dwindled along with his fighting force. And doubts about his leadership crept through the ranks.

George had lost New York City. Fearing the new nation's capital was next, his army raced toward Philadelphia.

The British kept up the chase through New Jersey, attacking constantly.

Traveling with the sick and wounded made escape impossible.

George watched as the patriotic spirit faded and men lost the will to fight.

By the time they crossed into Pennsylvania and set up winter camp, he had less than three thousand able soldiers. And in two weeks, at years-end, many would go home, their service complete.

George had to act while he still had men to fight.

Vowing

"VICTORY OR DEATH,"

George and his troops slipped through darkness, crossed an ice-filled river, and attacked the enemy.

With victory the fighting spirit returned! Soldiers signed up for another year. And more men enlisted!

But George's renewed hope soon turned to dread.

Recruits marching to winter camp brought smallpox on clothing, equipment, and inside themselves . . .

A horrible, undeniable truth echoed within George—smallpox was inescapable.

His only chance was to defeat it.

For weeks George agonized . . .

Inoculation illness was milder, safer . . .
but his army would be defenseless against attack.

Inoculation provided protection forever . . .
but thousands would be at risk if quarantine failed.

Inoculation could save his army . . .
or destroy it.

Finally George was convinced. The only way to break free from the disease was mass inoculation.

But HOW?

With little combat in winter, George needed fewer able-bodied troops. He devised a plan and launched his offensive.

Inoculate every soldier without immunity!

NOW!

Month after month thousands of men rotated through inoculation, quarantine, and recovery. New recruits underwent the procedure at enlistment sites, before marching to camp.

George demanded DISCIPLINE! SECRECY!

Without both . . . DISASTER!

Snow melted, muddy roads dried, and scouts reported enemy troops on the move.

George rushed orders to incoming troops.

The Continental Army fought through summer and fall, barely hanging on. When they straggled into Valley Forge the next winter . . . smallpox returned.

George took a count of men without immunity.

There were still thousands!

George refused to surrender to the disease.

He tightened control. He set up hospitals outside Valley Forge—the first stop for ALL incoming troops.

NO excuses.

NO delays.

NO ONE enters camp
without immunity!

George's plan worked!
At last he had the army he needed to defeat the British.
Disciplined. Trained. IMMUNE!

AUTHOR'S NOTE

George Washington's inoculation program against smallpox not only resulted in stronger, healthier troops but also contributed to creating a more skilled military as men served longer and gained valuable experience. Each winter he inoculated more soldiers against the disease. Though they battled the British for five more years, smallpox no longer had the power to destroy his army.

That difficult decision to inoculate his troops is considered by some experts to be Washington's most important strategic decision of the war. With his system of military hospitals, medical care, and the first government mass inoculation effort in American history, George Washington laid the foundation for public health in the United States.

The Continental Army's experience with smallpox taught Americans about inoculation and brought improvements in the procedure. After the revolution the public began to accept inoculation. In 1796, Edward Jenner created the first smallpox vaccine by using a similar virus that created immunity but didn't cause illness or contagion in humans. This breakthrough made smallpox vaccination safe and easy, and it became a tool to fight the disease worldwide. The global effort to eliminate the disease through vaccination reached its goal in 1980.

Though medicine has made huge advances since Washington's time, epidemics continue to affect lives around the world. The COVID-19 pandemic in 2020 made it clear that we too are part of history as school, work, and daily activities changed in response to the spreading virus. Like Washington's battle against smallpox, our experience showed the value of cooperation and unified action.

DIGGING INTO THE PAST WITH QUESTIONS

As I researched George Washington, smallpox, the Continental Army, the war, and life during the revolution, I worked to put the puzzle pieces together. The more I learned, the more questions I had. Here are a few you might be wondering about:

HOW DID GEORGE WASHINGTON GET SMALLPOX?

In 1751 nineteen-year-old George went to Barbados with his half-brother Lawrence who was ill with tuberculosis. They hoped the warm climate would improve Lawrence's health. While there, George caught smallpox. His diary has twenty-four days without entries while he suffered through the disease.

WHY DIDN'T THE AMERICAN COLONISTS USE INOCULATION TO CONTROL SMALLPOX LIKE THE BRITISH DID?

The colonists had known about inoculation for a long time. Cotton Mather, the main promoter of the procedure in Boston, had learned about it from Onesimus, a West African man he enslaved.

Smallpox outbreaks in the colonies were infrequent, so inoculation didn't seem worth the risks. Since few people had immunity, unsupervised inoculation could easily cause an epidemic. Inoculation could also cause death. Many American colonists rejected the procedure out of fear. And this fear led to riots, protests, and bans.

Also only the rich could afford the procedure, and few people had enough money to live without wages for a month while recovering.

George Washington urged his wife Martha to get inoculated. She resisted for a while but finally underwent the procedure in Philadelphia in May 1776. George visited

Finding the Small pox to be spreading much and fearing that no precaution can prevent it from running through the whole of our Army, I have determined that the troops shall be inoculated. . . . Necessity not only authorizes but seems to require the measure, for should the disorder infect the Army in the natural way and rage with its usual virulence we should have more to dread from it than from the Sword of the Enemy.

—George Washington
in a letter to William Shippen, Jr.,
February 6, 1777

her briefly in the hospital. Immunity allowed Martha to spend much of the war in army camps assisting with copying letters, tending the sick and wounded, and comforting troops.

WHAT OTHER DISEASES AFFECTED SOLDIERS DURING THE REVOLUTIONARY WAR?

While smallpox was the deadliest disease of the time, others such as malaria, yellow fever, dysentery, measles, typhus, typhoid, and scarlet fever also sickened troops. Ten times more soldiers died of disease than from war wounds.

RESOURCES

Visit George Washington's Mount Vernon online. Educational resources include videos, primary source documents, and more. mountvernon.org/education.

SELECTED BIBLIOGRAPHY

Quotations used in the book can be found in the following sources marked with an asterisk (*).

PRIMARY SOURCES

Ford, Worthington C., Gaillard Hunt, John C. Fitzpatrick, Roscoe R. Hill, Kenneth E. Harris, and Steven D. Tilley, eds. *Journals of the Continental Congress, 1774–1789: Friday, June 16, 1775*. Washington, DC, 1904–37: 92.

*Founders Online. "The Papers of George Washington." National Archives, founders.archives.gov/?q=Project%3A%22Washington%20Papers%22&s=1511211111&r=1.

*Rush, Benjamin. *The Autobiography of Benjamin Rush: His "Travels Through Life" Together with His Commonplace Book for 1789–1813*. Princeton: American Philosophical Society, 1948.

SECONDARY SOURCES

American Battlefield Trust. "Ten Crucial Days Campaign Dec. 25, 1776–Jan. 3, 1777," battlefields.org/learn/topics/ten-crucial-days-campaign.

———. "The Ten Crucial Days: A Second Success at Trenton," battlefields.org/learn/articles/ten-crucial-days-second-success-trenton.

———. "The Ten Crucial Days: December 24, 1776–January 3, 1777," battlefields.org/learn/articles/ten-crucial-days.

———. "The Ten Crucial Days: The Path to Trenton," battlefields.org/learn/articles/ten-crucial-days-path-trenton.

Becker, Anne M. "Inoculation in Washington's Army: The Battle against Smallpox." In *Science in Uniform, Uniforms in Science: Historical Studies of American Military and Scientific Interactions*, edited by Margaret Vining and Barton C. Hacker, 15–32. Lanham, MD: Scarecrow Press, 2007.

———. "Smallpox at the Siege of Boston: 'Vigilance against this most dangerous Enemy.'" *Historical Journal of Massachusetts*, 45 (Winter 2017): 43–75.

———. "Smallpox in Washington's Army: Strategic Implications of the Disease during the American Revolutionary War." *Journal of Military History* 68, no. 2 (April 2004): 381–430. jstor.org/stable/3397473.

Blanco, Richard L. *Physician of the American Revolution: Jonathan Potts*. Garland, NY: Garland STPM Press, 1979.

Ellis, Joseph J. *His Excellency: George Washington*. New York: Knopf, 2004.

Fenn, Elizabeth A. *Pox Americana: The Great Smallpox Epidemic of 1775–82*. New York: Hill and Wang, 2001.

Geppert, Cynthia, and Reid A. Paul. "The Shot That Won the Revolutionary War and Is Still Reverberating." *Federal Practitioner* 36, no. 7 (July 2019): 298–99. National Library of Medicine, ncbi.nlm.nih.gov/pmc/articles/PMC6654165/.

Gibson, James E. *Dr. Bodo Otto and the Medical Background of the American Revolution*. Menasha, WI: Collegiate Press, 1937.

———. "The Role of Disease in the 70,000 Casualties in the American Revolutionary Army." *Transactions & Studies of the College of Physicians of Philadelphia* 4, vol. 17 (1949–1950): 121–27.

Gillett, Mary C. *The Army Medical Department, 1775–1818*. Washington, DC: Center of Military History, US Army, 1981.

Kotowski, Peter. "Barbados." In *The Digital Encyclopedia of George Washington*, edited by Anne Fertig and Alexandra Montgomery. Mount Vernon Ladies' Association, 2012–. mountvernon.org/

library/digitalhistory/digital-encyclopedia/article/barbados/.

MacDonald, James. "Appointment as Commander in Chief." In *The Digital Encyclopedia of George Washington*, edited by Anne Fertig and Alexandra Montgomery. Mount Vernon Ladies' Association, 2012–, mountvernon.org/library/digitalhistory/digital-encyclopedia/article/appointment-as-commander-in-chief/.

National Park Service, Boston National Historical Park. "Smallpox, Inoculation, and the Revolutionary War," nps.gov/articles/000/smallpox-inoculation-revolutionary-war.htm?utm_source=article&utm_medium=website&utm_campaign=experience_more&utm_content=small.

Seidel, Maria. "Morristown, NJ." In *The Digital Encyclopedia of George Washington*, edited by Anne Fertig and Alexandra Montgomery. Mount Vernon Ladies' Association, 2012–, mountvernon.org/library/digitalhistory/digital-encyclopedia/article/morristown-nj/.

Stockwell, Mary. "Siege of Boston." In *The Digital Encyclopedia of George Washington*, edited by Anne Fertig and Alexandra Montgomery. Mount Vernon Ladies' Association, 2012–, mountvernon.org/library/digitalhistory/digital-encyclopedia/article/siege-of-boston/.

———. "Valley Forge." In *The Digital Encyclopedia of George Washington*, edited by Anne Fertig and Alexandra Montgomery. Mount Vernon Ladies' Association, 2012–, mountvernon.org/library/digitalhistory/digital-encyclopedia/article/valley-forge/.

Thacker, Brenda. "Disease in the Revolutionary War," In *The Digital Encyclopedia of George Washington*, edited by Anne Fertig and Alexandra Montgomery. Mount Vernon Ladies' Association, 2012–, mountvernon.org/library/digitalhistory/digital-encyclopedia/article/disease-in-the-revolutionary-war/.

Thompson, Mary V. "Smallpox." In *The Digital Encyclopedia of George Washington*, edited by Anne Fertig and Alexandra Montgomery. Mount Vernon Ladies' Association, 2012–, mountvernon.org/library/digitalhistory/digital-encyclopedia/article/smallpox/.

Werther, Richard J. "George Washington and the First Mandatory Immunization." *Journal of the American Revolution*, October 26, 2021. allthingsliberty.com/2021/10/george-washington-and-the-first-mandatory-immunization/.

ACKNOWLEDGMENTS

For each book, many people play a role as a story makes its way from idea to publication. This book wouldn't be possible without treasured institutions like the Library of Congress and the National Archives and all they offer. Tremendous gratitude goes to authors and historians Elizabeth Fenn and John U. Rees for vetting the manuscript. To critique partners Julie, Lynn, Ann, and Vivian—thanks for your valuable feedback along the way. My continued appreciation goes to literary agent Stephanie Fretwell-Hill and editor Carolyn Yoder for making this path possible. And so much love to my family who encourages, supports, and inspires me.

Calkins Creek
An imprint of Astra Books for Young Readers,
a division of Astra Publishing House
astrapublishinghouse.com
Printed in China

ISBN: 978-1-6626-8124-0 (hc)
ISBN: 978-1-6626-8125-7 (eBook)
Library of Congress Control Number: 2025944909

First edition

10 9 8 7 6 5 4 3 2 1

Design by Barbara Grzeslo and Michelle Mayhall
The text is set in Gill Sans and Caslon Antique.
The illustrations are set in watercolor, gouache, watercolor powder, colored pencils, and Neocolor crayons on Fabriano Artistico cold press natural white paper.

For the healers and
scientists who fight the battles
to keep us well
—BA

For Sarah, fellow artist and
forever friend
—AY